Body Language Proficiency

Terms and Conditions

Table Of Contents

Foreword

Body language is another form of subtle communication often practiced consciously or unconsciously. This "language" is fast gaining the interest of many people. Body language though very relevant but can sometimes be wrongly interpreted, however it is still useful.

Body Language Mastery

Master Human Psychology By Reading The Way People Behave With Their Bodies

Chapter 1:

Synopsis

There are many form of communication and sometimes a person's body language can actually indicate more things than the spoken word. Learning to understand body language can be very beneficial both in the work environment as well as on a more personal front. Body language reveals personal feelings and reactions to other people's feelings. However is has yet to be proven to be a science form and is not a real indicator to anything as it can be and is often manipulated.

The Basics

Most powerful people use this form of the unspoken word to make judgment calls which have proven to be a very effective way of getting and giving information. Some quarters qualify any and all movements in the body to be categorized as body movement; while others go even further to say that even breathing techniques fall in this category too.

When meeting someone for the first time, it is often a benefit to be able to read their body language signals to assess either the person or situation.

However again it may not be the best way to form an opinion because as mentioned earlier, body language can be manipulated. The art of body language is constantly being exchanged and interpreted between people on different levels of alternative communication.

While an individual is busy reading the body language of those he or she in interacting with, they at the same time are also reading the individual's body language. People who make it a habit of reading body language sign always have the advantage over any situation the thus having some knowledge on this subject would be good.

Chapter 2:

Synopsis

In order to be able to read the various body language signals fairly accurately, one must first have a basic knowledge of all the possible positions and meanings attached and projected by these various poses.

The Put Offs

When a person's demeanor personifies confidence the body language projected would be a brisk and erect walk. This movement successfully conveys the image and mind set of someone focused and sure of themselves.

The classic stance of hand on hips and legs slightly apart typical of people trying to portray authority actually reads as being ready for any outside reaction and potential aggression tendencies. It can also be used as an intimidating tool.

Sitting with legs slightly apart for men signals confidence and a very relaxed demeanor. This body language interpretation also applies to sitting with hands clasped behind the head and legs crossed or stretched out.

The open palm position shows sincerity, openness, and innocence, as does an easy slight smile or slight upturned corners of the mouth.

When it comes to the negative body language signs, unfortunately there are a lot to choose from and fairly easy to see and interpret. For instance, sitting with legs crossed and foot kicking slightly clearly signifies boredom while the arms crossed at the chest tells of an individual's defensiveness.

Walking with hands in pockets and shoulders hunched slightly, is a clear indication of dejection. Touching or slightly rubbing of the nose area is most commonly seen as rejection, doubt or lying. Rubbing the eye which is unwise to say the least could simply signify tiredness or feeling sleepy or have a more in depth sign of doubt and disbelief.

Anger and frustration are usually shown as clasped hands behind the back and a stiff spine position. Sometimes apprehension is also portrayed this way.

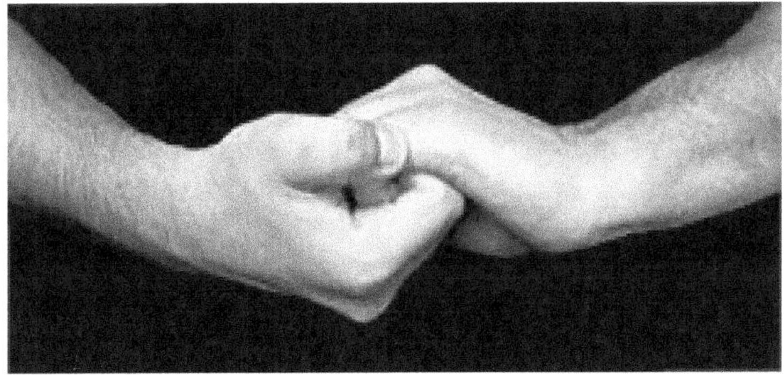

Chapter 3:

Synopsis

Being alert to reading the various non verbal signals people constantly give out in the form of body language is a very advantageous thing to be able to do. Fortunately it is not that hard to do and some people are even very easy to read as they are very open an expressive.

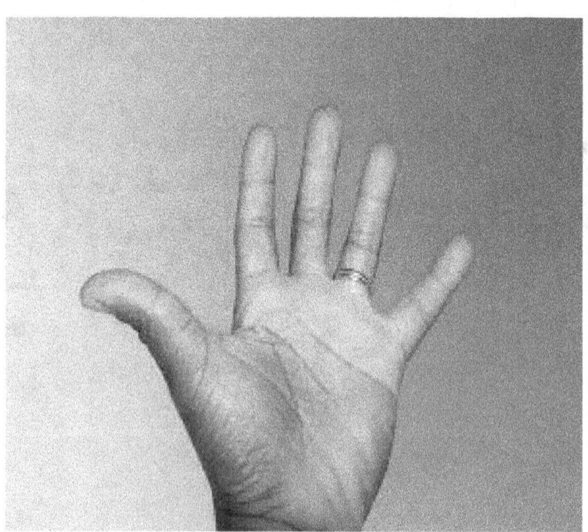

Watch

However learning to be attentive to these sometimes very subtle movements does require some practice and understanding. People who are not in tuned to their surrounding are less like to be sensitive to the body language. Purposefully and intently being conscious of the various body reactions will allow for further understanding of the person or situation.

Most reactions can be comfortably put into two distinct categories. The positive reaction and the negative reaction, however the interpretations may not always be as accurate as thought of.

For instance standing closer to another person could be interpreted as being comfortable and familiar with the said person, while the action of standing further away maybe perceived as being slightly aloof or simply being less comfortable or not wanting to encourage a closer relationship.

Though all equally natural assumptions it could be totally wrong for other less obvious reasons like perhaps the perfume or scent used by an individual is overpowering and thus quite disconcerting.

Another commonly interacted body language sign is the openness to being hugged or kissed. This particular action clearly shows the person's personality or their lack of. In being able to read this, those around are able to either extend the action or use a more reserved form of body contact.

When trying to gauge a situation or a new personality to an already existing group of people, the reactions spoken or implied through body language is very helpful.

The body language of the new comer is also going to be reflected in the corresponding reactions of those already established in the particular scenario.

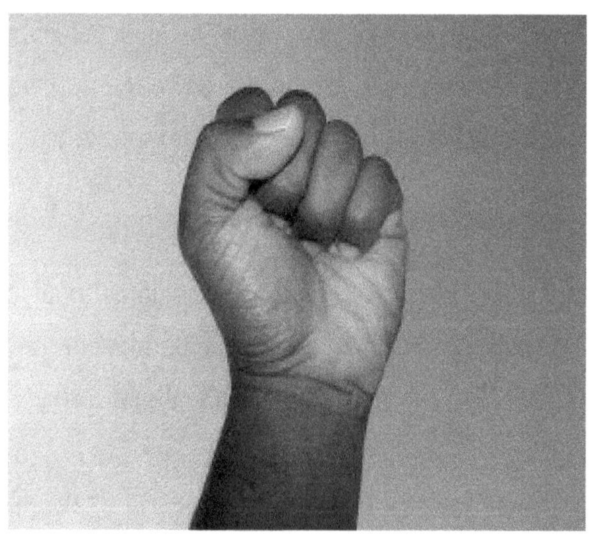

Chapter 4:

Synopsis

Most people come to a point in life when they desire to make a complete change to project a new image. After being the old out dated image for so long and finding only boring lifestyle to suit it, the idea of change is more than welcome.

Accomplishing

In order to do this rebranding exercise on one's self there has to be a certain clear cut goal to work towards. This is to ensure that the exercise is completed to the end and successfully. Some of the areas worth exploring are personal style, choice of clothing, personal body conditions are just a few to mention.

Changing the personal style of an individual is almost always the first goal to achieve in an overall make over. The general habitual body language should be able to be complimented with the change or adjustment of the personal style.

Having a good personal style will eventually transcend into the ability to make eye contact confidently and thus further portray the confidence in the body language too.

The overall dressing of an individual is also linked to the personality and body language practiced. People who generally prefer to be casually dressed give the impression of being easy going when coupled with the corresponding body language of a much laid back demeanor.

In contrast those who are always impeccably dressed have a rather stiff body language. If the idea is to be more professional in demeanor than the corresponding image should also project this.

For some, the original habit of poor grooming is a norm. If there is to be some form of interaction with others especially in a more friendly way then the issue of personal grooming should be addressed.

Having an image in mind of the desired outcome is the first step to actually considering and changing the overall demeanor of the individual through new and more appropriate body language signals.

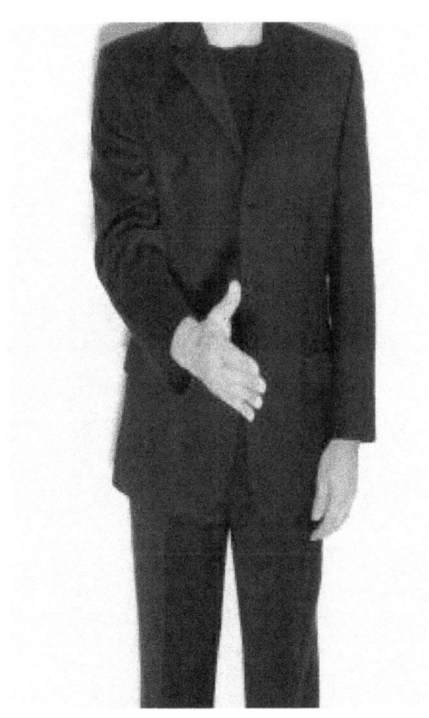

Chapter 5:

Synopsis

Today almost everything is taken at face value and for most; this way of reading people is not only beneficial but fairly quick. However the danger is the wrong interpretations could be read and thus the wrong idea formed.

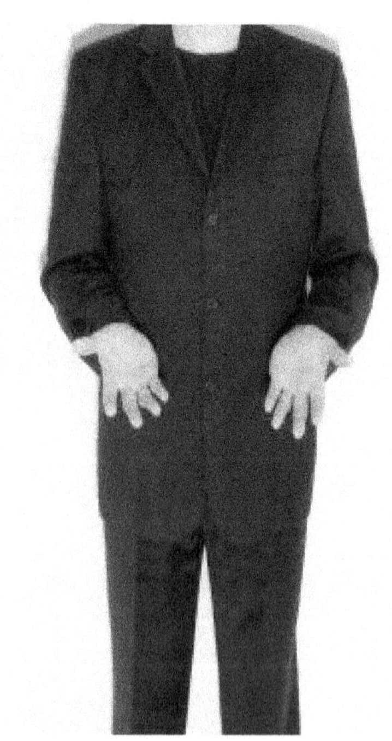

Rehearse

Life is like a stage and to get anywhere everyone must play the game cooperatively. Most people have a habit of practicing some body language routines in front of a mirror. This is a good way to see what other people are seeing and to make the necessary changes to ensure the right messages are getting across through the body language used.

Practicing scenes in the mirror also allows for the individual to gain the necessary confidence in the proposed encounter which he or she is practicing for. This then also ensure the body and facial movements portray the desired results and not to be misconstrued.

Sometimes people unwittingly portray the exact opposite of what they actually mean to and this can cause unnecessary problems for all parties involved. Body language is subtle form of getting the message across and there is certainly a need to be sure that the message is not assumed or presumed.

Therefore by practicing the various different poses and expressions in front of a mirror the mind can actually disseminate what the eye perceives.

Once the desired body language action and facial contours are mastered, the individual will be able to have a new found confidence in actually replaying it all at the appropriately appointed time. This confidence is apparent because the mind's eye has already been privy to the personified confidence shown by the mirror image. Also subconsciously the person becomes more aware of the "new" image rather than the "old" image when actually playing out the intended practiced role.

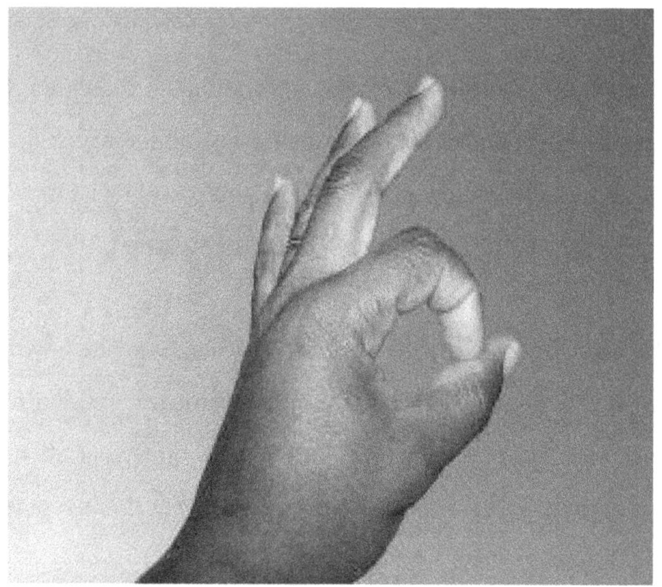

Chapter 6:

Synopsis

As already firmly established, body language is a very important stubble form of communicating feelings and reactions to the surroundings. Also previously established is the fact that body language can also be manipulated to an advantage or required circumstances.

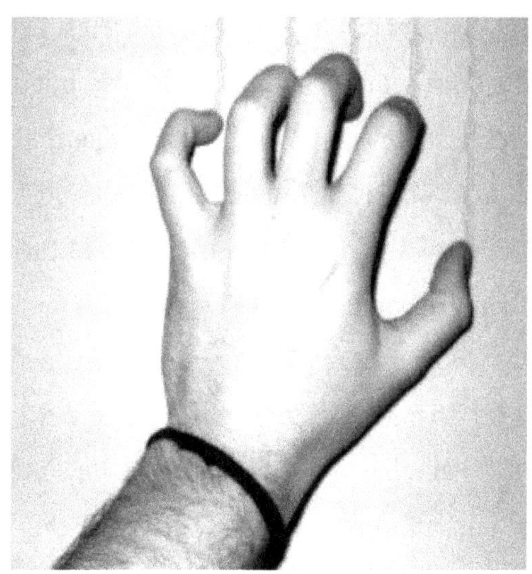

The Right Way

Here are some areas where one can train or manipulate the body to react in a certain way in order to achieve the desired results.

• Eye contact – this is an important aspect to be mastered when dealing with people. Ensuring constant eye contact allows the recipient to be assured that there is some level of interest in what is being discussed. Whether feigned or not eye contact is something worth learning to exercise. It also makes the recipient feel more at ease and confident in the situation.

• Posture is another important body position that dictates not only the actual feeling of tiredness and being drained but also physically causes these feelings to manifest itself. This is due to the hunched or droopy shoulders as well as the hunched positions all contributing to the inhibition of good and deep breathing. This in turn will give the impression of being uncomfortable or nervous.

• Using the head positions to dictate the perceived body language message is also another effective way of making a situation comfortable or uncomfortable. Tilting the head slightly while talking or listening implies a friendly demeanor while keeping the head ramrod straight and aligned with the back and spine implies seriousness and even annoyance.

• The all popular crossing of arms clearly indicates disapproval from time beginning. Commonly done from an authoritive position it tells everyone to back off and give the individual space. On the other hand, hands hanging loosely or kept behind the back implies being in control and able to take on anything, which is a good body language to develop to project the desired effects.

Chapter 7:

Learn How To Take Down Someone's Wall with Positive Body Positions

---

Synopsis

Sometimes when verbal communication does not work, one has to find other alternatives to get the message across effectively and quickly. Everyone has their own distinct ways of expressing themselves and those who are familiar with the body language signs will have no problems interpreting these signals.

The Way To Get In

In order to create a comfortable situation or improve an otherwise uncomfortable situation the use d of different body language positions can help. These various positions are used to create the desired difference in how people receive the implied messages, the general mood of the recipient or even to strike a balance in those around.

Some commonly practiced and recommended body positions that can help keep those around feeling at ease and even happier are as follows:

• Smiling – this very rarely brings on a negative response or reaction. Most people will almost immediately change their negative responding reaction to a positive one, when a smile is offered. It would be hard to respond to a smile with a harsh negative reaction.

• A confident sitting position is also another way to "shake" any negative elements in both the individual and those around. Giving the impression of being relaxed yet with a certain amount of alertness, the individual will be able to defuse any possible responsive slouching individuals. It also encourages those around to be an energetic as possible with the straight upright position.

• In practicing slower and more precise moments the individual is also creating a sense of calmness all around. This in turn will also encourage those around to be equally calm and relaxed.

All these when put into practice regularly until it becomes fairly natural will cause those around to be positively affected too. When this is accomplished the percentage of confrontations is lessoned and kept under control.

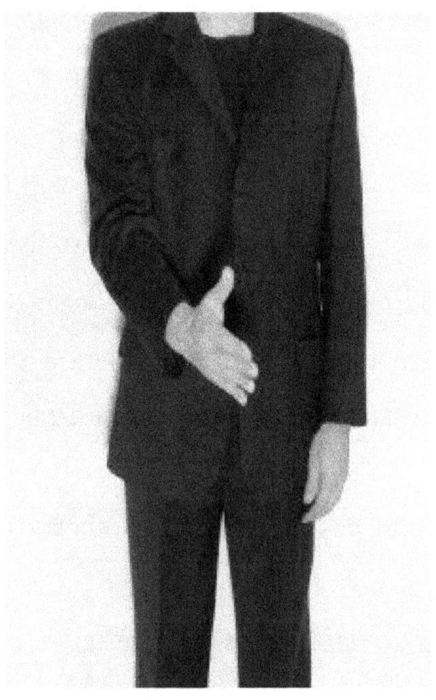

Chapter 8:

Understand The Importance Of Symmetry

Synopsis

Achieving symmetry in life is a goal worth working towards. In life all things must have some sort of balance. Technically symmetry patters help us organize out little individual worlds conceptually. For the even more technically discerning individual, symmetry is best explained as an occurrence in nature and the inversions by artists, craftspeople musicians, choreographers, and mathematicians.

Equal

For the individual however this is more than just striking a balance. Going by the general rule that in all things there is an action and a reaction would be a simpler way to explain this rather too simply implied term. Being able to react or cause a certain reaction is in some way exercising some control over the outcome of any given situation.

If an individual wishes to engage in a scenario where upon the outcome is beneficial to all, then the relevant body language needs to be focused and specifically tuned towards the said outcome. The response to the practiced and planned different body language should have the intention of achieving some level of symmetry in its delivery.

Sometimes or perhaps most times the symmetry of any situation needs to be readjusted in order to gain the reflection intended or desired.

If the desired symmetrical reaction needed and desired is meant to be positive, then the corresponding body language should be done in a way that engages the same positive reflective results.

Sending out the body signals that personify the positive aura will almost always be able to achieve the positive outcome that is symmetrical in nature. The same would apply to the oppositely generated body language.

Technically the symmetrical system can be broken up into a few distinct parts which are rotation symmetry, reflection symmetry, translation symmetry and glide reflection symmetry. All of these can be inter related and reflected in the various corresponding body language.

Chapter 9:

Understand The Importance Of Matching The Other Person

Synopsis

In all settings most people go out of their way to be accommodating and receptive to the needs of others. Unfortunately this has slowly become a dying state of art to practice.

Some Suggestions

In the various hectic and self focused scenarios today people sometimes lose sight that their individual actions and speech patterns don't just affect themselves but also affects those around.

In some cases the consequences are so far reaching, that it is sometimes difficult to understand how an action or word which is perceived to be a small insignificant gesture can have monumental effects.

Body language can have this unusual reflective result. The only important thing to bear in mind is that whatever body language being exercised will have some reaction or another.

Therefore the idea behind the practice of controlling the intended body language movements should always be to garner the positively intended results.

Creating a comfortable or uncomfortable situation, intentionally or unintentionally is always the idea behind trying to match the others around, through the use of body language.

This is an effective tool that is sometimes much more effective that using the power of the spoken word. It has been said, either in jest or in seriousness that "looks can kill" or "actions speak louder than words." Though the latter does not really or specifically refer to the actual actions there are some connotations that can be linked to it.

In always considering the actions and body language practices, it would be advantageous to a certain extent as this is indeed a very effective tool to use both in an individual's personal and professional life.

In social settings too the use and manipulation of the body language to garner the intended reflective response is very much depended upon the execution style of the said body language.

Chapter 10:

What You Can Get Into With The Incorrect Body Language

Synopsis

Often time people don't realize the impact of the body language and its consequences on any given particular situation or scenario.

Some Facts

Most people breeze through the day without this reality ever coming the light. However for the discerning and some would sad intelligently scheming few, the purposeful use of body language in the daily life has proven to be quite an effective and beneficial tool.

Practicing to be consciously and continually aware of this sometimes very effective tool is an art worth exploring. However on the other hand the wrong or subconscious use of the body language tool can bring about unnecessary and sometimes annoying results. Incorrect use of body language can bring about the reactions and reflections that are not needed or wanted and thus causing a great inconvenience to both the person suing the body language too and the perceived receiver. Such misinterpretation can end up causing the almost opposite intended reactions.

Especially in relationships when a particularly innocently termed body language is exercised and reflected the consequences of said actions can and often are wrongly perceived, resulting in the very messy process of trying the "straighten" everything out. In business too, a wrong perception of the body language tool can cause very damaging results indeed. Therefore it is indeed prudent to practice to be ever conscious of the body language being implied and practiced. This is indeed necessary to avoid any unnecessary inconveniences from occurring.

Wrapping Up

There are a lot of positive results that can be gotten from the practiced use of positive body language. But in order to understand and acquire the skills to consciously practice the positive body language tactics, one first has to have some basic knowledge of the actual expressions and actions involved.

In doing so there is a good possibility in being able to avoid the consequences of incorrect body language signals or actions being reflected in a person's demeanor either consciously or subconsciously.